TAKE TEN YEARS

1950s

Library of Congress Cataloging-in-Publication Data

Sharman, Margaret.
    1950s / Margaret Sharman.
        p.   cm. — (Take ten years)
    Includes bibliographical references and index.
    Summary: Explores the decade of the 1950s worldwide, discussing such topics as the war in Korea, Joe McCarthy, the Soviet power struggle, civil rights activities, and Castro in Cuba.
    ISBN 0-8114-3078-2
    1. History, Modern—1945- —Juvenile literature. [1. History, Modern—1945–] I. Title.   II. Title: Nineteen-fifties.
III. Series.
D842.5S52   1993
909.82′4—dc20

92–25916
CIP
AC

Typeset by Multifacit Graphics, Keyport, NJ˙
Printed in Spain by GRAFO, S.A., Bilbao
Bound in the United States by Lake Book, Melrose Park, IL
1 2 3 4 5 6 7 8 9 0 LB 97 96 95 94 93 92

Acknowledgments

Maps — Jillian Luff of Bitmap Graphics
Design — Neil Sayer
Editors — Caroline Sheldrick, Shirley Shalit

For permission to reproduce copyright material the author and publishers gratefully acknowledge the following:

Cover photographs — UPI/Bettmann; Popperfoto; © The Estate of Elvis Presley

page 4 — The Hulton Picture Company, Harry S. Truman Library, Topham, UPI/Bettmann Newsphotos, Associated Press/Topham; page 5 — Popperfoto, Science Photo Library, Popperfoto, UPI/Bettmann, The Vintage Magazine Company; page 8 — Topham; Page 9 — Popperfoto; page 10 — (top) AP/Wide World Photos, (bottom left, right) Popperfoto; page 11 — The Hulton Picture Company; page 12 — (left) Popperfoto, (right) UPI/Bettmann; page 13 — (top left) Archive Photos, (top right, bottom) Popperfoto; page 14 — Topham; page 15 — (top) Popperfoto, (bottom) UPI/Bettmann; page 16 — UPI/Bettmann; page 17 — (top) Popperfoto, (bottom) Agence Nature/NHPA; page 18 — Topham; page 19 — (left) The Vintage Magazine Company (right) UPI/Bettmann Newsphotos; page 20 — (top, bottom) Popperfoto; page 21 — United States Air Force; page 23 — (left, right) Popperfoto; page 24 — Popperfoto; page 26 — (left) Popperfoto, (right) UPI/Bettmann Newsphotos; page 27 — (top left and right) The Hulton Picture Company, (bottom) AP/Wide World Photos; page 29 — (top, bottom) Popperfoto; page 30 — (left) Springer/Bettmann Film Archive, (right) AP/Wide World Photos; page 31 — (top, middle) Popperfoto, (bottom) Topham; page 32 — UPI/Bettmann; page 33 — (top left) Springer/Bettmann Film Archive, (top right) Popperfoto, (bottom) Science Photo Library; page 34 — (left) Popperfoto, (right) The Vintage Magazine Company; page 35 — Popperfoto; page 36 — (left, right) UPI/Bettmann; page 37 — (left) The Vintage Magazine Company, (right) Photofest/Retna Pictues Ltd; page 38 (top) AP/Wide World Photos, (bottom) Popperfoto; page 39 — Popperfoto; page 40 — Popperfoto; page 41 — (top) Popperfoto, (bottom) AP/Wide World Photos; page 42 — (left) UPI/Bettmann, (right) The Vintage Magazine Company; page 43 — (left) Topham, (right) Popperfoto; page 44 — (1, 2) The Vintage Magazine Company, (3, 4, 5) The Advertising Archives; page 45 — (1, 2) The Vintage Magazine Company, (3) © 1959, General Motors Corporation. Reproduced with permission of General Motors Corporation/Advertising Archives, (4) The Advertising Archives, (5) The Vintage Magazine Company, (6) The Advertising Archives.

TAKE TEN YEARS

1950s

MARGARET SHARMAN

RSVP
**RAINTREE
STECK-VAUGHN**
P U B L I S H E R S
The Steck-Vaughn Company

Austin, Texas

Contents

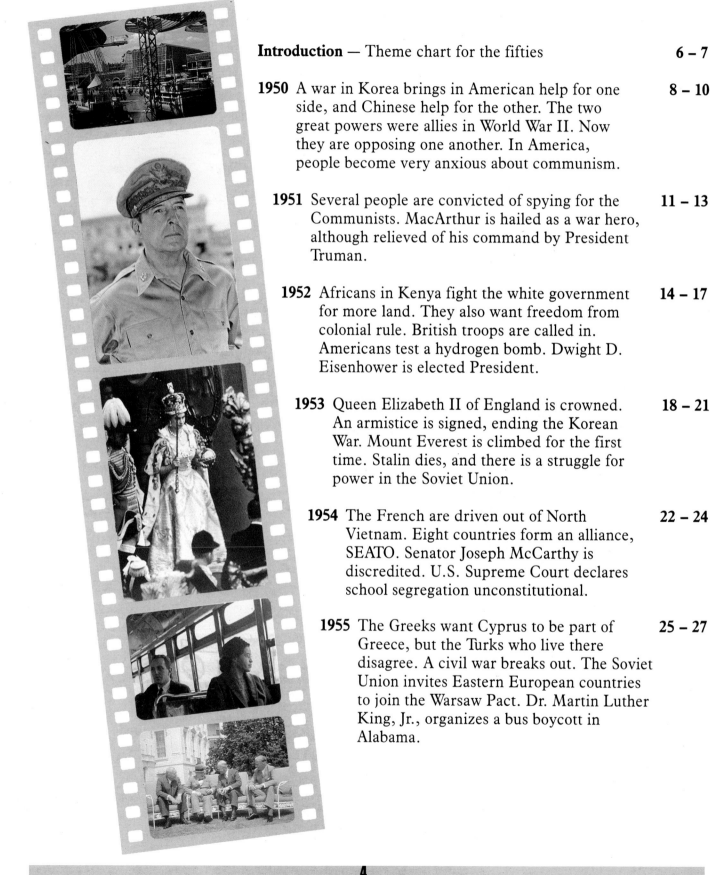

The pictures on page 4 show
The Festival of Britain site, London
Douglas MacArthur
Queen Elizabeth II's coronation
Rosa Parks on Montgomery bus
Churchill (second from left), with Eisenhower, Eden, and
    Dulles, outside the White House, Washington

The pictures on page 5 show
Khrushchev, Bulganin, and Eden
Sputnik I
The first troops to arrive in Port Said
Some of first American astronauts
Fidel Castro

Introduction

In 1950, the effects of World War II were still present. Major European cities had been badly bombed, and new houses, factories, and stores had to be built. Food in some areas was still in short supply, and some rationing continued.

The United States had not been as devastated by the war as Europe, and rationing had ended. However, 400,000 Americans had died. And while many American families were still grieving, another area of bitter conflict opened up in Korea. Also, although the threat of Nazism was over, Americans now saw communism as the new hated and feared enemy.

There was much unrest in countries occupied by foreign rulers. In Africa, the British granted independence to the Gold Coast, and it became Ghana. Kenyans struggled for freedom and more land in a guerrilla war known as the Mau Mau rebellion. The Egyptians seized the Suez Canal, which the British and French had controlled for 75 years. The French had to leave Vietnam, and also faced guerrilla fighters in Algeria. The Tibetans resisted the Chinese, and the Hungarians tried to rid themselves of the Russians.

Many of these conflicts could have led to a third world war, as the superpowers took opposite sides. The dreadful threat of nuclear weapons may have averted war. Also, the United Nations was able to defuse some dangerous conflicts. But between East and West, a deadly "Cold War" raged. Toward the end of the decade this nerve-racking Cold War had thawed a little, but several smaller countries were still danger spots.

It was also a decade when people reached out for new knowledge. Nuclear power plants began to create electricity, but at the same time H-bombs were tested. People were nervous about the threat of nuclear war. Nobody wanted that. They were encouraged by the spectacular achievements in a new direction: the Russians launched the world's first artificial satellite, and Americans trained astronauts for space flight. It seemed as if science fiction was coming true.

YEARS	WORLD AFFAIRS
1950	U.S. and USSR are rivals; the U.S. is afraid of Communist power in the East.
1951	The Cold War: trials of suspected spies Baudouin becomes king of Belgium.
1952	Coup in Egypt UN headquarters completed. U.S. scientists test deadly H-bomb.
1953	Queen of England crowned. Power struggle in USSR when Stalin dies Tito becomes president of Yugoslavia.
1954	Nasser leads Egyptian republic. SEATO formed. Vietnam to be divided into two countries.
1955	Warsaw Pact signed. South Vietnam becomes a republic.
1956	Nasser takes over Suez Canal. Cold War begins to thaw.
1957	Gold Coast becomes Ghana. European Common Market formed. Russians launch Sputniks.
1958	General de Gaulle is premier of France. Egypt and Syria become the UAR. King Feisal of Iraq is murdered.
1959	Castro takes over in Cuba. The space race is on. Dalai Lama flees from Tibet.

WARS & REVOLTS	PEOPLE	EVENTS
The North Koreans invade South Korea.	McCarthy accuses people of being Communists. Frank Sinatra sings in London.	The Stone of Scone is stolen. Holy Year celebrated at the Vatican. McCarran Act passed.
MacArthur pushes back North Koreans and wants to march into China; President Truman dismisses him.	Maclean and Burgess disappear from British Foreign Office. Perón reelected president of Argentina.	U.S. gets permission to build air bases in England.
Mau Mau uprising in Kenya	Dr. Linse abducted in Berlin. Eisenhower elected President.	Olympic Games in Finland Coelacanth discovered. Buckminster Fuller's geodesic dome house displayed.
East German revolt Armistice ends Korean War.	Hillary and Tenzing climb Everest. Watson and Crick discover DNA. Dr. Salk develops polio vaccine.	Pilot Jacqueline Cochran breaks sound barrier. Earl Warren becomes Chief Justice.
French fight North Vietnamese.	Roger Bannister runs mile in less than 4 minutes. Oppenheimer not allowed to work on atomic projects.	Supreme Court declares school segregation unconstitutional. Atomic submarine launched.
Civil war in Cyprus	Dr. Martin Luther King, Jr., leads fight against prejudice. Albert Einstein dies.	Bus boycott in Alabama Disneyland opens in California.
Hungarians revolt against Russian rule. Conflict over Suez Spanish demonstrations against Franco	Grace Kelly becomes a princess. Eisenhower reelected President.	Olympic Games in Australia *Under Milk Wood* performed. *My Fair Lady* is hit in New York.
	Beatniks in U.S.A. and England Althea Gibson wins tennis championships at Wimbledon.	Central High School in Little Rock, Arkansas, admits black pupils under direction of federal troops sent by President Eisenhower.
Civil war in Algeria Americans and British land troops in Jordan.	Pope John XXIII crowned. Elvis Presley joins army. Pasternak wins Nobel Prize.	NASA opened in U.S.A. Jet service to Europe begins. Franco frees political prisoners.
Coup in Cuba More trouble in South Vietnam Mau Mau rebellion is over.	Khrushchev visits America. Charles van Doren wins quizzes by fraud. Makarios is president of Cyprus.	Russians photograph other side of the moon. Alaska and Hawaii become 49th and 50th states.

1950

THE WAR IN KOREA

NORTH KOREANS INVADE SOUTH

June 25, The Far East Korea is divided into two countries. North Korea is a Communist republic. South Korea is a Democratic republic. The boundary between the two is the line of latitude 38°, known as the 38th parallel.

Today 60,000 North Korean soldiers, with Russian tanks and jet planes, crossed the 38th parallel, and invaded South Korea. The invasion has alarmed the Western powers. The United States helped South Korea after World War II. The USSR and the United States seem to be taking opposite sides in this dispute.

UNITED NATIONS STEPS IN

June 30, South Korea The North Korean army has captured South Korea's capital, Seoul. The South Koreans do not have an effective Army, and their weapons are out of date. The United Nations has asked its members to help South Korea. The first American troops arrived today.

GENERAL MACARTHUR TAKES COMMAND

July 7, South Korea General MacArthur of the United States is commander of all forces in South Korea. Jet planes are bombing Pyongyang, the Northern capital. But the strong North Korean forces are resisting the UN army.

AMERICANS FORCED BACK TO PUSAN

Sept. 1, South Korea The UN forces, mostly Americans, have been pushed right back to Pusan, on the southeast coast. Today they were joined by British troops. Their enemies, the North Koreans, began a terrific bombardment today along a 50-mile (80-km) front. The war is not going well.

UN troops in action in Korea.

A SECOND FRONT IS OPENED

Sept. 15, South Korea Over 250 ships have arrived at Inchon, on the west coast. They are troop carriers bringing in U.S. soldiers. The country around Inchon is held by their enemies, the North Koreans. The U.S. soldiers will fight their way towards Pusan. This will not be easy; the roads are mined and the opposition is very great. But it means that the enemy has to fight two armies.

UN FORCES ON THE OFFENSIVE

Oct. 9, South Korea The troops from Inchon managed to reach Pusan. The two armies fought their way north and recaptured Seoul. Today they crossed the 38th parallel.

There is now a new threat, this time from China. President Chou En-lai said the UN troops had no right to invade North Korea.

UN FORCES HAVE TO WITHDRAW

Oct. 27, North Korea At least 14 Chinese divisions have crossed into Korea. The UN forces are heavily outnumbered. Russian MIG planes are bombing their positions. They are retreating back towards the 38th parallel.

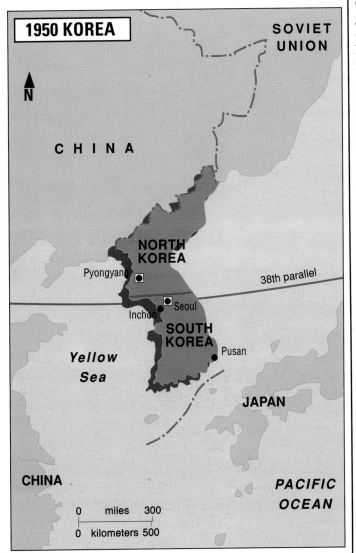

Korea is divided at the 38th parallel.

UN FORCES FACE DEFEAT

Dec. 24, South Korea The UN army has lost all the ground it gained. A huge number of Chinese troops were sent against the Allies on November 26 and 27. But MacArthur believed that the Allied forces outnumbered the Chinese. He also counted on our air power to keep more Chinese from entering North Korea. He was confident that the war would be over by Christmas. However, by December 4, the superior numbers of Chinese troops forced the Allies to begin retreating. About 105,000 U.S. and Korean troops are being evacuated by sea.

CROWDS RECEIVE POPE'S BLESSING

July 9, Vatican City This is Holy Year for Roman Catholics. From all over the world pilgrims are coming to Rome. Today Pope Pius XII blessed the huge crowd of pilgrims from an upper window of his residence in Vatican City.

His Holiness Pope Pius XII.

SENATOR SEES REDS EVERYWHERE

Feb. 20, Washington A British nuclear scientist, Dr. Klaus Fuchs, has admitted that he supplied atomic secrets to the Russians. Suddenly Americans realize that the Russians may be making atomic bombs too. They are frightened of a nuclear war. Senator Joseph McCarthy is taking advantage of their fear. He accuses over 200 people in the State Department of being secret Communists. He gives no proof of this, but people believe him.

McCARRAN ACT PASSED

Sept. 9, Washington Senator McCarthy's powerful anti-Communist campaign today received important support. Congress passed the Internal Security Act. This Act was sponsored by Senator Patrick McCarran of Nevada. It gives the government close control over all Communists and their activities in this country. Some people fear that the Act will lead to widespread suspicion and unfounded accusations.

NEWS IN BRIEF . . .

A STONE DISAPPEARS

Dec. 29, Scotland The Stone of Scone is missing. It came from Scotland in 1296 and was placed under the coronation chair in Westminster Abbey, London. Britain's monarchs are crowned over this stone. An anonymous letter says the thieves will tell where it is, but only if it can be kept in Scotland.

NEAT AND SMART IS FASHIONABLE

Spring, Paris Nylon stockings are as popular as ever. They are held up with garters from the new elastic roll-on girdles. These are a perfect foundation for Dior's sheath dresses and tailored skirts. For dancing, wide skirts over several petticoats are set off by a wide belt. Blouses are soft nylon. Makeup is very important for eyes and lips. Nail polish matches the lipstick.

Young men on the dance floor wear suits and ties. Chain stores, with branches in every town, can supply a ready-to-wear suit for under $15. A girl likes her escort to be stylish.

AMERICAN BREAKS RECORD

Aug. 8, Calif. American swimmer Florence Chadwick has broken a 24-year-old record for swimming the English Channel. The earlier record was set by another American woman, Gertrude Ederle, when she swam the channel in 1926 in 14 hours, 31 minutes. Miss Chadwick shaved the record by a little over an hour, making the swim in 13 hours, 20 minutes. The first person to swim the channel without a life jacket was Matthew Webb, who in 1875, swam it in 21 hours, 45 minutes.

SINGER DELIGHTS HIS FANS

July 15, London Frank Sinatra is singing to packed audiences in London this week. He is the most popular singer in the United States. Bing Crosby once said, "He has the voice of a lifetime—but why did it have to happen in mine?"

1951

SPIES AND SUSPECTED SPIES

HISS'S APPEAL FAILS

March 12, Baltimore For two years, Alger Hiss has denied charges that he spied for Russia. He was never found guilty, but last year a court did find him guilty of lying under oath. He was sentenced to five years. Hiss appealed, but today the court refused to reduce his sentence. People still wonder if he was in fact a spy.

FOREIGN OFFICE MEN DISAPPEAR

June 8, London Two senior British Foreign Office officials, Donald Maclean and Guy Burgess, have been missing since Friday, May 25. On the following Monday, officers from the British secret service were going to question Maclean. They suspected him of spying for the USSR. The government is wondering whether someone warned Maclean. Police are searching for them.

POLICE QUESTION A THIRD MAN

Nov. 30, Washington An inquiry has opened into the Burgess and Maclean affair. A diplomat named Kim Philby was recalled from his job at the British Embassy here to answer questions. Guy Burgess stayed in Philby's house. As a senior British Foreign Office official, Philby knew Maclean was going to be questioned in May. The inquiry found nothing to suggest that he was guilty.

ROSENBERGS FOUND GUILTY

April 5, New York Julius Rosenberg and his wife Ethel have been sentenced to death for spying. They are accused of obtaining information about the atomic bomb in 1944. David Greenglass, who worked on the bomb project, passed information to Rosenberg. He passed it on to an agent named Harry Gold. Greenglass and Gold confessed, but the Rosenbergs said they were innocent. The Rosenbergs are Communists. Their lawyer says they cannot get a fair trial because of Senator McCarthy's anti-Communist activities.

Julius and Ethel Rosenberg after their trial.

GIs HEAD FOR ENGLAND

June 18, Washington Now that the British government has given its permission, the U.S. will proceed with plans to build a permanent air base for fighter and bomber planes in England. Residents near the planned base are not happy about this.

FESTIVAL A TONIC TO THE NATION

June 1, London The Festival of Britain is raising spirits with its color and fun. All along the South Bank of the Thames River, mud flats have been drained and old houses pulled down. In their place is an elegant collection of buildings. A magnificent new concert hall seats 3,000 people. The biggest dome ever built covers the Dome of Discovery. It is like a mushroom on thin legs. There is a crazy railroad and a children's zoo. The tall thin needle is called the Skylon. It is lit up at night, and is a symbol of the future. The Festival Gardens and funfair are extremely popular. This is the first large leisure park in Britain.

The Festival of Britain site with the Skylon.

MACARTHUR GETS HERO'S WELCOME

April 20, New York Today, riding in a motorcade here, Douglas MacArthur was given a hero's welcome on his return from Korea. Huge crowds cheered. Signs reading "Welcome Home" and "Well Done" floated overhead.

This was in spite of the fact that on April 11, President Truman removed MacArthur from all his Far East commands because he wanted to march his men into China. The President feared this action might start a third world war.

BELGIANS WELCOME KING BAUDOUIN

July 16, Brussels King Leopold III of the Belgians has abdicated (resigned). The Belgians think he should not have surrendered to the Germans in 1940. There have been riots and strikes against him. His very popular first wife, Queen Astrid, died in a car crash in 1935. Her elder son will become King Baudouin I.

SPANIARDS WANT THEIR ROCK BACK

Aug. 5, Barcelona Today has been proclaimed Gibraltar Day. Gibraltar, site of the famous Rock of Gibraltar, has been a British possession since the 17th century. The Spanish say that it is part of Spain. They will mark this day every year until they get the "Rock" back.

WOMEN WORKERS BREAK RECORD

November, Washington More American women are employed at paying jobs than ever before. The number is estimated at about 19,300,000. Much of this growth began in World War II. About 18 million women worked in war industries. While men reclaimed many of these jobs, the trend toward female employment continued.

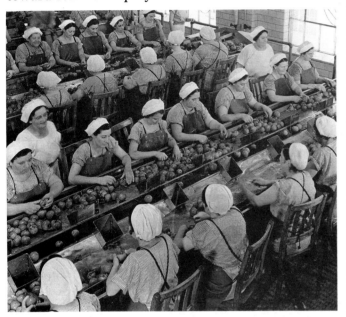

Women workers inspecting tomatoes for a soup-canning company. They are cutting out the damaged parts.

PERÓN BACK IN POWER

Nov. 11, Buenos Aires, Argentina Colonel Juan Perón has been reelected president of Argentina. He first came to power in 1945. Perón is very popular with working people. His wife Eva (Evita) has worked tirelessly among them. Her influence has won him many votes at election time. But the economy of the country is weak, and Perón has an added burden: his wife is very ill with cancer.

Juan and Eva Perón wave to the crowd at Buenos Aires.

NEWS IN BRIEF . . .

FAMILY LIFE TODAY

Sept. 30, Chicago Many towns are spreading outward as houses are built in the suburbs. Most new houses are being equipped with central heating that is fueled by oil or by gas instead of coal. Most of these suburban homes are being bought by young couples with children. Usually the husband goes out to work while his wife looks after the children and does the housework. Many more people are marrying young these days.

GOOD FAMILY ENTERTAINMENT

Dec. 15, New York Singing cowboy Gene Autry has swept to fame with a song that is out just in time for Christmas. The new song is called "Rudolph the Red-Nosed Reindeer." Home entertainment is booming. The number of TV sets has increased. As a result 3,000 movie theaters have had to close. The movie industry has to produce better films to keep its audience. This year Marilyn Monroe has made *The Asphalt Jungle* and Bette Davis stars in *All About Eve*. There are drive-in theaters in many areas. From your car, you can watch the movie on a huge screen.

On a night out at a drive-in movie.

1952

MAU MAU IN KENYA
AFRICANS WANT MORE LAND

Jan. 1, Nairobi At the beginning of this century, British settlers were given farms in Kenya. They enclosed their lands and would not allow strangers onto them. This is against African custom. Africans say that land belongs to everyone. Their population has increased, partly because of European medicine. Available land has become scarce.

A group of black nationalists has formed the Kenya African Union (KAU). They want the white government to give Africans more land. The nationalists sing a song which, translated, means: "Mother, whether you cry or not, I will only come back when our lands are returned; when I obtain our lands and African freedom."

OATH-TAKING IN KIKUYULAND

Aug. 24, Nairobi A secret society called Mau Mau is recruiting Africans of the Kikuyu tribe. Recruits are forced to swear an oath that they will murder people if asked to. The Kikuyu believe that oaths are very powerful, and they will die if they break one. Most recruits are too frightened to protest. Oath-givers are touring the Kikuyu districts near Nairobi, recruiting for Mau Mau.

FUNERAL OF KIKUYU CHIEF

Oct. 14, Nairobi Sir Evelyn Baring (the governor of Kenya), Jomo Kenyatta (the president of the KAU), and members of the government were among the hundreds of mourners at the funeral of Kikuyu Chief Waruhiu. A week ago three gunmen shot him dead. Police believe the gunmen were Mau Mau, who have already murdered over 40 Kikuyu. A few days before his death Chief Waruhiu condemned Mau Mau violence.

Jomo Kenyatta (in light trousers) pictured at the funeral ceremony of Chief Waruhui. Mr. Kenyatta is president of the KAU and is also suspected of being a Mau Mau leader.

STATE OF EMERGENCY IN KENYA

Oct. 21, Nairobi A state of emergency has been declared in Kenya. British troops are coming in. They will search for the Mau Mau terrorists, who are living in the forests and hills. Others who have taken the Mau Mau oath stay in the towns. They supply the terrorists with food and information. Town dwellers suspected of being Mau Mau have been rounded up.

Kenyatta was arrested. The British government thinks that the KAU is organizing Mau Mau.

British troops guard Kenyan villagers during a search for Mau Mau hidden weapons.

FULLER'S GEODESIC DOME DISPLAYED

Aug. 30, New York On display today at the Museum of Modern Art was designer Buckminster Fuller's new geodesic dome house. This prefabricated structure combines great strength with light weight. It is built with a framework of aluminum tubes covered by a weatherproof plastic "skin." Living areas are hung from the framework by strong cables. The model on dipslay here represents an 80-foot dome. However, Mr. Fuller claims that it is possible to build an 800-foot dome that would weigh only 1,000 tons. It could be quickly taken apart and rebuilt at another site.

PROMINENT WEST GERMAN ABDUCTED

July 8, West Berlin Berlin is surrounded by East Germany. The city is divided between the Russians, the Americans, the French, and the British. Dr. Walter Linse, a lawyer living in Berlin, has told people about the cruelty taking place in East Germany. Today Dr. Linse was kidnapped in broad daylight. He was shot in the leg and bundled into a car. East German guards at the border closed the barrier after the kidnap car had passed.

The East Germans have put up double barbed wire fences along the frontier with West Germany.

Architect Buckminster Fuller in front of one of his full-sized geodesic structures.

KING FAROUK TOLD TO LEAVE

July 23, Cairo There has been a coup in Egypt. A group of young army officers has deposed King Farouk. Their leader is called Jamal Abdel-Nasser. King Farouk lived in luxury, and did not tackle his country's problems.

The rebels have set up a Revolutionary Council. General Neguib, head of the armed forces, will lead it. The Council will expel Europeans from top government jobs. They want the British army to leave the Suez Canal Zone. The British are alarmed at these decisions.

HEROES OF THE OLYMPICS

Aug. 3 Helsinki, Finland On July 19 a 55-year-old runner lit the Olympic torch to open the Olympic Games. The Finns gave him a great welcome. In 1920 and 1924 he was their Olympic hero. His name is Paavo Nurmi. He still runs.

The Russians took part in the games for the first time since 1912. Two of their female competitors won gold medals. But this year's hero was Emil Zatopek of Czechoslovakia. He created Olympic records for the marathon, and the 10,000 and 5,000 meter events. Jerome Biffle of the U.S. won the long-jump contest.

A young woman dressed in white tried to take advantage of this meeting of East and West. At the opening ceremony she ran forward to plead for world peace. She was turned away from the microphone, her message unspoken.

NEW BOMB WILL BE DEADLY

Nov. 1, Washington United States scientists wore special dark glasses to watch tests on a new atomic bomb. The bomb is hundreds of times more powerful than those dropped on Japan in 1945. It is called an H-bomb (H is for hydrogen). Radioactive dust rose in a huge cloud 24 miles (40 km) high and 100 miles (160 km) wide. The tests were carried out on an uninhabited island in the Pacific. After the explosion, the island had completely disappeared. The Russians may also be working on an H-bomb. Some people are building bomb shelters.

EISENHOWER ELECTED PRESIDENT

Nov. 3, Washington Dwight D. Eisenhower, once supreme commander of the Allied Expeditionary Force in World War II, has been elected President of the United States. Eisenhower, a Republican, won by a wide margin over Democratic candidate Governor Adlai E. Stevenson of Illinois. The popular vote was about 34 million to 27 million. It seems that most Americans admire and trust Dwight Eisenhower. They also rely on him to protect them from the threat of communism. Eisenhower's vice-president will be California senator Richard Nixon.

Eisenhower campaigning from the back of a train in St. Joseph, Missouri.

NEWS IN BRIEF . . .

OPERA GAINS A NEW WORK

Feb. 28, London Benjamin Britten conducted his new opera, *Billy Budd*, this month at Covent Garden Opera House. The opera takes place on board an 18th-century naval ship. It tells the sad story of a sailor who accidentally kills an officer who is tormenting him. The tenor Peter Pears sings the leading role.

UN HEADQUARTERS COMPLETED

Fall 1952, New York The buildings of the United Nations headquarters have finally been completed. Located on land along the East River, construction began in 1948, after Congress approved a large interest-free loan to finance the project. The major buildings are the Dag Hammarskjold Library, the General Assembly Building, and the Secretariat Building, a striking skyscraper. The UN began in 1945, with 50 nations pledging to work for world peace.

A NEW WORLD CHAMPION

Sept. 24, Philadelphia Rocky Marciano is now the new world heavyweight boxing champion. Last night he knocked out "Jersey" Joe Walcott after 13 rounds. In the first round Rocky was behind on points. But he recovered, and used his hard-hitting technique to batter the former champion. Rocky learned to box in the army during the war. Before he took up boxing seriously, his first love was baseball.

3-D MOVIES HERE TO STAY?

Nov. 26, Los Angeles Movie-goers have to wear special glasses to see the latest movie, *B'wana Devil*. One lens is red, the other green. The glasses make the film seem to be three-dimensional. This could cause panic—in *B'wana Devil* lions appear to leap out of the screen! We shall see whether 3-D movies catch on, or if this is just a new gimmick.

A NEW DAVY CROCKETT

July, Nashville, Tenn. These days, Senator Estes Kefauver is wearing a coonskin cap as he chats with potential voters. In his bid for the Democratic presidential nomination, the liberal senator from Tennessee is using this colorful Davy Crockett headgear as his trademark in the campaign.

UNUSUAL FISH IS RARE SURVIVAL FROM STONE AGE

Dec. 29, Madagascar A fisherman has caught a very strange fish in the Indian Ocean. It is called a coelacanth. Fossil remains of the fish have been found in rocks. Scientists thought the fish became extinct about 50 million years ago!

1953

A QUEEN IS CROWNED

June 2, London The New Elizabethan Age began today when Queen Elizabeth II was crowned in Westminster Abbey. Her golden coach was drawn by eight white horses. At the climax of the long ceremony, the Archbishop of Canterbury put the crown on her head. One royal visitor pleased the London crowd above all others. This was Queen Salote of Tonga, an island in the Pacific. Her warm personality and beaming smile drew cheers from the onlookers.

All over the country people are attending street parties and band concerts. In the evening most towns have dances and firework displays. It has been a cold, rainy day, but this has not dampened the general excitement.

ARMISTICE AGREEMENT SIGNED

July 27, Panmunjom, Korea An armistice was finally signed here today, ending the Korean War. The signers were an American general who represented the United Nations and a Korean general representing the North Korean and Chinese Communist forces. There will be a neutral zone between North and South Korea about 2.5 miles (4 km) wide, and prisoners of war will be exchanged.

The cost in lives and property of this conflict has been enormous. Almost 500,000 Americans fought in this war. Almost 160,000 were killed or wounded. The U.S. spent over $65 billion on the war. Much of Korea was badly damaged and both Koreas suffered huge numbers of deaths.

CLIMBERS ON ROOF OF THE WORLD

May 29, Nepal At 11:30 this morning two climbers made history. Edmund Hillary of New Zealand, and Tenzing Norgay of Nepal have reached the summit of Mount Everest. Sir John Hunt led the party of 10 British and 36 Nepalese climbers. Yesterday Hillary and Tenzing camped at a point nearly 27,900 feet (9,000 meters) up the mountain. The temperature was –16°F, and the wind rose at times to gale force. At the top of Everest, Tenzing buried gifts of food to the god of the mountain, and Hillary buried a small crucifix.

Edmund Hillary (left) and Tenzing Norgay on Everest.

JOHN FITZGERALD KENNEDY WEDS

Sept. 12, Newport, R.I. Senator John F. Kennedy of Massachusetts, married Jacqueline Lee Bouvier here today. The Most Reverend Richard J. Cushing, Archbishop of the Archdiocese of Boston, performed the ceremony at St. Mary's Roman Catholic Church. He read a special blessing from the pope. A reception for 1,200 was held at the bride's family estate, Hammersmith Farms. Guests included several senators and governors.

THE VIEW FROM EVEREST

"I was beginning to tire a little now. I had been cutting steps continuously for two hours and Tenzing, too, was moving very slowly . . . I wondered rather dully just how long we could keep it up . . . I then realized that the ridge ahead, instead of still monotonously rising, now dropped sharply away . . . A few more whacks of the ice-axe in the firm snow and we stood on top.

My initial feelings were of relief—relief that there were no more steps to cut—no more ridges to traverse and no more humps to tantalize us with hopes of success. I looked at Tenzing and in spite of the balaclava, goggles and oxygen mask all encrusted with long icicles that concealed his face, there was no disguising his infectious grin of pure delight as he looked all around him. We shook hands and then Tenzing threw his arm around my shoulders and we thumped each other on the back until we were almost breathless. It was 11:30 a.m."

Edmund Hillary, from *The Ascent of Everest* by John Hunt, Hodder & Stoughton 1953

NEW PRESIDENT RESISTS SOVIETS

Jan. 13, Belgrade, Yugoslavia Josip Tito has become president of Yugoslavia. He is the country's first Communist president. Stalin wanted Yugoslavia to be under Soviet control. Tito has resisted him. Yugoslavia will remain a neutral country—though its policies are like those of the USSR.

AFRICAN LEADER IS EXILED

Nov. 30, Kampala, Uganda The Kabaka (king) of Buganda, Mutesa II, has been forced to leave Uganda by the British. Buganda is the country of the Ganda people. It forms a quarter of the British territory of Uganda. When self-government comes, the Ganda want Buganda to be a separate country. They are furious that their king has been exiled.

President Tito of Yugoslavia at his villa home.

TANKS HALT EAST GERMAN REVOLT

June 21, Berlin The East Germans live under Soviet rule. They have gone on strike against longer hours of work, and the low standard of living. Thousands of German prisoners of war are still in Russia. The rioters demanded their return. They tore down Communist flags in the city.

It is the first time a country has revolted against Soviet occupation. Usually people are too frightened to do so. The Russians have sent tanks into the streets of East Germany to restore order.

SCIENTISTS FIND "SECRET OF LIFE"

April 25, Cambridge, England We have known for some years that our height, looks, brain power, and everything about us depends on our genes. We inherit our genes from our parents. J.D. Watson and F.H.C. Crick of the University of Cambridge have discovered that genes are made of a chemical called DNA. DNA has a structure like a twisted ladder, which splits in half when a cell divides.

Demonstrators in East Berlin attack Soviet tanks.

VILLAGERS MASSACRED IN KENYA

Sept. 15, Lari village, Kenya After a long trial, Jomo Kenyatta has been sentenced to seven years hard labor. He denied he was leading the Mau Mau, and his arrest has not stopped their attacks. They have destroyed 150 schools and killed 32 teachers. Last night they murdered nearly 100 men, women, and children by setting fire to a whole village.

Many Kikuyu are against the Mau Mau. They have joined the Kikuyu Guard to protect their families. They show great bravery, because Guard posts are obvious targets for Mau Mau attacks.

USSR HAS NO FIRM LEADER

Dec. 23, Moscow Stalin's death on March 5 was followed by a power struggle in the USSR. At that time Lavrenti Beria, the chief of the secret police, had immense power. But so had other leaders, including Molotov, Malenkov, and Khrushchev. Beria is the first one to "disappear." Malenkov accused him of being a Western spy and trying to seize power. Today he was executed. The Russians hardly care who finally becomes sole leader. Forced labor, concentration camps, and the dreaded secret police still dominate their lives.

NEWS IN BRIEF . . .

SEARCHING THE SEA BED

Jan. 15, Switzerland A 70-year-old Swiss scientist, Auguste Piccard, has dived in a bathyscaphe of his own design to the bottom of the Mediterranean. He reached a depth of 2 miles (3.5 km). The fish down there live in total darkness. Professor Piccard has explored not only the depths but also the heights: 22 years ago he reached the stratosphere in a huge hydrogen-filled balloon.

WOMAN BREAKS SOUND BARRIER

May 18, Los Angeles Today pioneer pilot Jacqueline Cochran became the first woman to break the sound barrier. She flew a jet over Edwards Air Force Base at speeds over 760 miles per hour. In 1938, she was the first woman to fly in the Bendix Trophy Race, which she won. In World War II, she formed and commanded the Women Airforce Service Pilots. Jacqueline Cochran became the first American civilian woman to be awarded a Distinguished Service Medal.

CRIPPLING DISEASE ATTACKED

March 26, New York The most feared disease today is poliomielitis (polio). Many victims die. Some have to use an "iron lung," which helps their paralyzed lungs to breathe. Others are crippled for life. Now at last a scientist, Dr. Jonas Salk, has vaccinated a group of children, to prevent them getting the disease.

WARREN IS NEW CHIEF JUSTICE

Sept. 30, Washington Governor Earl Warren of California has been chosen 14th Chief Justice of the U.S. Supreme Court. Congress is expected to approve President Eisenhower's choice. Mr. Warren is known as a liberal. However, even conservatives respect him for his honesty and devotion to the law.

1954

VIETNAM AND THE FRENCH
FRENCH HOLDING VIETNAM

Jan. 1, Dien Bien Phu, Vietnam Since 1945 the French have occupied a part of northern Vietnam. Vietnamese Communists, the Viet Minh, want the French to leave. Their forces are led by General Giap. The country around Dien Bien Phu is mountainous, and thickly forested.

Last November the French dropped paratroops in the northwest of Vietnam, and captured Dien Bien Phu. They thought that guerrillas would come down in small groups from the mountains, and be easy targets to attack. But General Giap was cleverer than that. He has led a huge army to the outskirts of Dien Bien Phu. His soldiers even dragged field guns over the mountains. And 20,000 men with equipment on bicycles followed through the narrow jungle paths. It is clear that General Giap means to oust the French garrison from its stronghold position.

VIET MINH ENTER TOWN

May 8, Dien Bien Phu After a siege lasting 55 days, the French have finally been defeated by the Viet Minh. The French garrison of about 19,000 men was completely surrounded. The French did not hold any of the territory around Dien Bien Phu, so there was nowhere for them to go. Those who survived the siege surrendered to General Giap's troops. It seems that after this heavy defeat, France has no future in Indo-China.

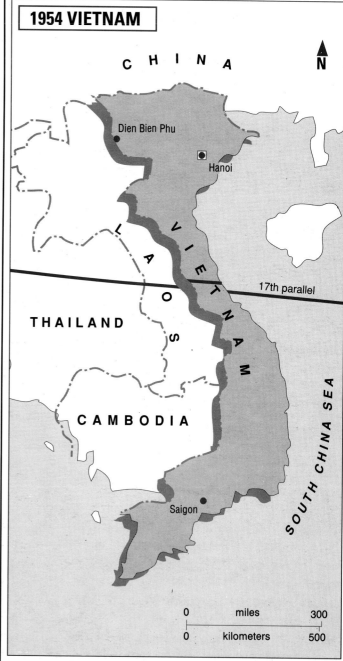

1954 VIETNAM

During the course of this year, Vietnam was divided into two countries and gained two new capital cities.

22

VIETNAM TO BE DIVIDED

July 21, Geneva The United Nations has ruled that Vietnam should be divided into two countries. The northern part, where all the fighting has taken place, is to be called North Vietnam. Its capital will be Hanoi. Ho Chi Minh, the Communist leader of the Viet Minh, will be its president. His rule will end at latitude 17°, the "17th parallel." South of this is South Vietnam. It will be ruled by Emperor Bao Dai. The French will support his government.

Ho Chi Minh, leader of the Viet Minh

FAMILIES MOVE TO THE SOUTH

Oct. 8, Vietnam Thousands of refugees are leaving North Vietnam and going to South Vietnam. President Eisenhower has sent American ships to transport them by sea. He says that Communist gains in southeast Asia have "a domino effect": when one country falls, the second, third, and fourth need less and less pressure to fall too. He does not like to see a Communist government in North Vietnam.

THE WITCH-HUNT IS OVER

Dec. 2, Washington Joseph McCarthy's fellow senators have finally turned against him. He has called too many innocent people Communist, or un-American. In the past four years he has charged two presidents with treason, threatened the army chiefs, and recruited hundreds of anti-Communist spies. Because of him 600 college professors have been dismissed.

SEATO AIDS PEACEFUL DEVELOPMENT

Sept. 8, Manila, Philippines Eight countries have agreed to join together to keep the peace in southeast Asia. They will also send southeast Asian countries money for their development. The members of SEATO (South-East Asia Treaty Organization) are the U.S., Britain, France, Pakistan, Australia, New Zealand, Thailand, and the Philippines. They will meet next year.

TROOPS TO LEAVE SUEZ

July 27, Cairo, Egypt The British have agreed that troops will leave the Suez Canal Zone over the next two years. They will only return if a Middle Eastern country tries to invade Egypt. The agreement was signed with Colonel Nasser. Last May he declared the country a republic. His policy to end imperialism is known to all Egyptians; his new radio station broadcasts his socialist and anti-Western views.

British troops beside the Suez Canal.

SEGREGATION IS UNCONSTITUTIONAL

May 17, Washington In the case of *Brown* v. *Board of Education of Topeka*, the Supreme Court today struck down an 1896 ruling that allowed separate public schools for Negroes and whites. This earlier verdict held that if the facilities for study were equal, segregation was not unconstitutional. Today the Court ruled unanimously that segregation was unconstitutional. Chief Justice Earl Warren said: "In the field of public education, the doctrine of separate but equal has no place."

It is expected that states in the South will be angry about this landmark decision.

THE POWER OF A NUCLEAR BLAST

June 29, Washington Last month the United States exploded another H-bomb. The test took place on the island of Bikini. The bomb's power was so great that fishermen in a boat 68 miles (112 km) away were badly affected by radiation sickness.

People all over the world are extremely frightened in case war breaks out between two countries with H-bombs. A leading American scientist, Dr. Robert Oppenheimer, would like to ban them. He helped to develop nuclear bombs. Now he is no longer allowed to work on atomic projects because of his anti-bomb views.

NEWS IN BRIEF . . .

ATHLETE IN FOUR-MINUTE MILE

May 6, Oxford, England For years runners have been trying to run a mile in less than four minutes. Finally today 25-year-old Roger Bannister has set a record of 3 minutes 59.4 seconds. He is very interested in the whole subject of running—how to get the best out of yourself. He trains carefully.

The exciting record-breaking moment as Roger Bannister crosses the winning line.

MAU MAU REVENGE

May 26, Kenya "Treetops," a noted tourist center, has been burned down by the Mau Mau. This act was in revenge for the British attempt to ambush a Treetops truck driver. The driver had been taking supplies and food from the tourist lodge to the Mau Mau terrorists in the mountains. The ambush failed. However, British Royal Air Force planes are now trying to bomb the Mau Mau out of the mountain range.

ATOMIC SUB LAUNCHED

Jan. 21, Groton, Conn. The first ship powered by atomic energy was launched here today. It is the U.S. warship *Nautilus*. The *Nautilus* is a 340-foot-long submarine, which cost $55 million to build. It has a top underwater speed of over 30 knots and can circle the earth without ever coming to the surface. The launching was attended by a crowd of over 12,000 people.

WHERE WINE FLOWS LIKE WATER

Oct. 15, France The grape harvest is attracting a lot of transient labor. The grapes are made into wine, which is one of France's most famous exports. It is also a Frenchman's daily drink. Doctors say a man should drink no more than two quarts of red wine a day. Many drink a lot more, especially in rural areas. The government is starting a campaign to warn people of the danger of heavy drinking.

1955

CIVIL WAR IN CYPRUS

ISLANDERS WANT UNION WITH GREECE

Jan. 1, Nicosia, Cyprus The island of Cyprus is ruled by the British. Although it lies just south of Turkey, more Greeks live here than Turks. Cypriot Greeks want Cyprus to be part of Greece. They call this union *enosis*. Five years ago they gained a powerful leader. He is Archbishop Makarios, head of the Greek Church in Cyprus. Athens radio encourages Cypriot Greeks to fight for *enosis*.

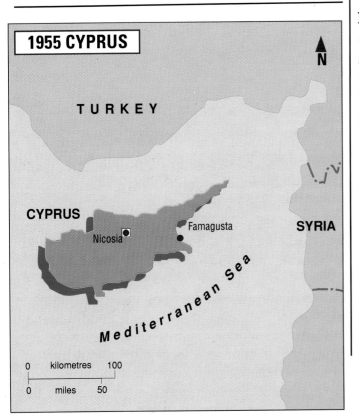

1955 CYPRUS

N

TURKEY

CYPRUS

Nicosia   Famagusta   SYRIA

Mediterranean Sea

0	kilometres	100
0	miles	50

FIGHTING BREAKS OUT IN CYPRUS

June 30, Nicosia A Greek army officer, Colonel George Grivas, has recruited hundreds of young Greeks into a guerrilla army. It is called EOKA, which in Greek stands for National Organization of Cypriot Struggle. They are burning buildings in Nicosia, the capital of the country, and in the eastern town of Famagusta. A large number of Turkish civilians have been murdered, and their homes and farms destroyed.

STATE OF EMERGENCY IN CYPRUS

Nov. 28, Nicosia The British government declared a state of emergency in Cyprus. This means that the governor may deport or arrest anyone who disturbs the peace. Only the British are allowed to be armed. This comes after months of heavy fighting. British commando troops were flown in. They have been searching for guerrillas in the mountains. Hundreds of people have already been arrested. If they are convicted of planting bombs or of murder they are executed.

There is still intense fighting in the streets of Famagusta. The troops are calling this the "Murder mile." The British blame Archbishop Makarios for supporting Colonel Grivas and the EOKA. This is one more British territory that is causing trouble. But if the British leave, the Greeks and Turks will still be quarreling. The British government hopes to solve the crisis first.

Although close to Turkey, Cyprus is a largely Greek island, under British rule.

THE WARSAW PACT SIGNED

May 14, Warsaw, Poland The Soviet Union and seven other Eastern European countries have made a pact to help one another. If one country is attacked, the rest will go to its defense. But they are agreed that disarmament is necessary for world peace. The Russians organized the Warsaw Pact as an association similar to NATO, the alliance to which Western countries belong. The headquarters of the Warsaw Pact is in Moscow.

The Warsaw Pact committee meets.

NEGROES BOYCOTT BUSES

Dec. 15, Montgomery, Ala. Negroes here have sworn to walk or cycle to work instead of going by bus. On December 1, Rosa Parks, a Negro dressmaker, got on a bus after work. She was tired and sat down in a "whites only" seat. The driver told her to move to the back. Montgomery law says that Negroes must sit in the rear of buses. This type of law is known as a "Jim Crow" law. It makes discrimination against Negroes legal. Rosa Parks refused to move and was arrested. Negro leaders are asking all Montgomery Negroes to boycott—refuse to use—the city's buses. A young Negro minister Dr. Martin Luther King, Jr., is to lead the city-wide boycott to protest Rosa Parks's arrest. Dr. King insists on nonviolent means of protest to force desegregation of the Montgomery city bus system.

MARIAN ANDERSON SINGS AT MET

Jan. 7, New York Contralto Marian Anderson tonight became the first Negro soloist in history to sing at the Metropolitan Opera House. She sang in Verdi's *A Masked Ball*. The great conductor Arturo Toscanini said that her voice is one "heard once in a hundred years."

Marian Anderson takes a bow after her performance at the Metropolitan Opera House.

SOUTH VIETNAM IS A REPUBLIC

Oct. 26, Saigon The emperor of South Vietnam, Bao Dai, lives in the south of France. He left the government of the country to his ministers. In April rebels started a civil war in Saigon, the capital. They defeated the government, and today they declared South Vietnam a republic. Its first president is Ngo Dinh Diem.

BURGESS AND MACLEAN NEWS

Guy Burgess   Donald Maclean

Sept. 18, London A Russian has published an article in a British newspaper. It is about the missing British Foreign Office men Guy Burgess and Donald Maclean. They are in the Soviet Union. The article claims they were recruited as Russian spies while they were at Cambridge University in the 1930s. Nobody has discovered yet who is the "third man" who warned them to leave England.

NEWS IN BRIEF . . .

LITTLE MO IS TO RETIRE

Feb. 22, New York Maureen Connolly is going to retire from tennis championships. She was only 16 when in 1951 she won the U.S. women's tennis tournament. In 1953 Little Mo, as she was called, became the first woman to win the "grand slam": the national championships of the United States, Great Britain, France, and Australia. Little Mo is a great horse rider. But last year she had a fall and injured her leg. She has not played in tennis tournaments since then. Now she plans to coach other talented players.

ACTOR KILLED IN ROAD ACCIDENT

Sept. 30, Los Angeles James Dean was the hero of countless teenage movie fans. He has died today in a car crash at the age of 24. His latest movie has not yet been released. Called *Rebel Without a Cause*, it is about a rich young man who is angry and frustrated with life. James Dean's death brings to an end a promising career, which began with a part in the movie *East of Eden*.

EINSTEIN DEAD AT 76

April 18, Princeton, N.J. Albert Einstein, one of the greatest scientists in history, died today. He is most famous for his theory of relativity. He published this in 1905, when he was 26. In this paper, he set forth the notion of the relativity of time. His theory has changed the world's ideas about space and time. In 1905, he wrote another important paper. It had to do with an idea about the nature of light. It led to the development of sound movies and television. A third 1905 paper supported the theory that all of the matter in the universe is made up of atoms.

Albert Einstein was born in Germany. He came to the United States in 1933 to escape the Nazis and became an American citizen in 1940.

Einstein at the Carnegie Institute in 1931.

DISNEYLAND OPENS

July 18, Anaheim, Calif. Walt Disney is famous for his cartoon characters, like Mickey Mouse and Donald Duck, and for his cartoon movies. Now he has opened a sensational theme park called "Disneyland." A world of make-believe, it cost about $17 million. Five million visitors a year are expected.

CROCKETT BOOM ENDS

Dec. 15, Montreal, Canada The craze for Davy Crockett hats is over. Christmas shoppers are looking for other attractions. The trade in coonskins boomed for six months as children dressed like their hero. The real Davy Crockett was an American hunter who died in 1836. His picture shows him dressed in a fur hat with a tail. Now the "King of the Wild Frontier" is becoming just a legend once more.

1956

THE SUEZ CRISIS

NASSER TAKES OVER CANAL

July 26, Suez, Egypt Colonel Nasser has nationalized the Suez Canal. He announced this after America and Britain decided not to pay for Egypt's new Aswan Dam. With the money the canal earns, the Egyptians will be able to pay for the dam themselves. The British and French say that Nasser's action is unlawful.

PILOTS WALK OUT

Sept. 14, Suez Today British and French pilots walked out of their jobs on the Suez Canal. The Egyptians have only a few trained pilots of their own. It is a highly specialized job. The Egyptian pilots say that they will work long hours without extra pay. They will train new recruits. Colonel Nasser says he will never use foreign pilots again.

ISRAELIS THREATEN EGYPT

Oct. 30, Suez Prime Minister David Ben-Gurion of Israel has sent troops toward the canal from the east. The purpose is said to be to keep the Egyptians from raiding Israeli territory. The British and French have demanded that both Israelis and Egyptians withdraw, leaving a no-man's-land of 10 miles (16 km) on each side of the canal. The Israelis have agreed, but the Egyptians have not.

EGYPTIANS BLOCK THE CANAL

Nov. 6, Suez The Egyptians have sunk several ships in the Suez Canal, and have completely blocked it. All ships will now have to travel around the Cape of Good Hope. This adds 6,000 miles (10,000 km).

British aircraft have bombed military targets in Egypt. The British and French dropped paratroops in the area. The Israelis are again advancing toward the canal. The United Nations has asked all foreign troops to leave Egypt immediately.

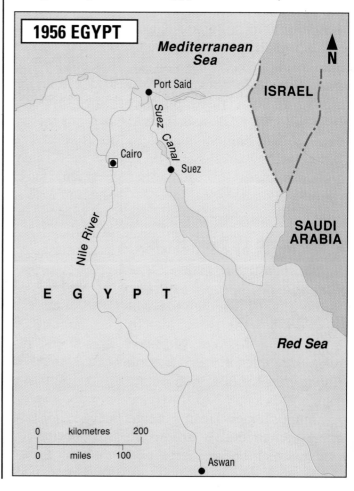

HUNGARY FIGHTS FOR FREEDOM

Oct. 31, Budapest, Hungary Last week a huge crowd of people gathered in Budapest's main square. They demanded that Russian troops leave Hungary. Since the war Russian secret police have been spying on Hungarians. Nobody had any freedom of speech or action. Now people have brought out national flags that have been hidden for years. They have destroyed a huge bronze statue of Stalin in the city center.

Rioters entered the prison and freed Cardinal Mindszenty, the head of the Roman Catholic Church in Hungary. He was sentenced by the Russians to life imprisonment in 1949.

Demonstrators in Hungary pulled down a huge statue of Stalin.

RUSSIANS RETURN IN FORCE

Nov. 5, Budapest After just five days of freedom, Hungary is once again under the Russian heel. Yesterday Soviet planes bombed the center of Budapest. A thousand tanks flattened houses and fired on civilians. Nikita Khrushchev, head of the Communist party, says that the troops were invited back by loyal Hungarian Communists.

The Hungarians fought bitterly and bravely, but they did not have the power to resist. Cardinal Mindszenty is safe in the American Embassy. Professional guides are charging high prices to lead over 200,000 refugees across the border into Yugoslavia and Austria. The route to freedom is dangerous because it is heavily mined.

UN FORCES ARRIVE AT SUEZ

Nov. 21, Suez A United Nations peacekeeping force has arrived at Suez to take over control of the region. It will take several months before the canal can be used again. The Americans blame the British for handling the affair badly.

The first UN troops arrive in Port Said, Egypt.

EX-CHIEF RETURNS TO AFRICA

April 8, Gaberones, Bechuanaland Seretse Khama has returned to the country of his birth, Bechuanaland (Botswana). In 1948 he married an English-woman, Ruth Williams. The marriage upset his people, the Bamangwato. Seretse Khama was going to be their chief. How could his son, who would be half English, succeed him? To avoid trouble, the British rulers exiled Seretse Khama from Bechuanaland. He now says he will give up the chieftainship. Ruth Khama is very happy to be returning to her adopted country.

EISENHOWER REELECTED PRESIDENT

Nov. 6, Washington Dwight D. Eisenhower has been reelected President of the United States. He won with an even greater margin than he did in 1952. "Ike" has always been liked and respected by the American people. Now it appears that they approve of the way he has been handling the Suez crisis. They also admire his courage in the face of his recent illnesses. We still "like Ike"!

MY FAIR LADY A HIT

March 15, New York The new Lerner and Loewe musical *My Fair Lady* opened to rave reviews on Broadway tonight. It was adapted from a play by famous Irish writer George Bernard Shaw. It is a story about a professor who turns a young street seller into a society lady. Among the hit songs is "I Could Have Danced All Night."

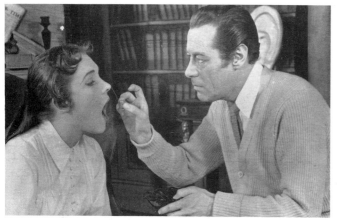

Julie Andrews and Rex Harrison in *My Fair Lady*.

STUDENTS STAGE FREEDOM MARCH

Nov. 29, Barcelona, Spain There have been student demonstrations in Spain. The students marched, carrying placards saying WE ARE AGAINST DICTATORSHIP—and below—FOR HUNGARY. They are really against General Franco's dictatorship in their own country. Everybody is under state control. Spaniards have to work harder than other Europeans for less pay. They cannot afford much to eat. They take great risks when they demonstrate against the state. Thousands of Spaniards have been imprisoned without trial.

COUNTRIES BOYCOTT OLYMPICS

Dec. 8, Melbourne, Australia The 16th Olympic Games opened here today, the first to be held "down under," in Australia. Several countries decided not to join in this year. They are protesting against Russia's invasion of Hungary, and Britain's and France's treatment of Egypt. But three African countries were represented for the first time: they are Kenya, Malawi, and Ethiopia. Harold Connolly of the United States won the hammer throw event.

Al Oerter of the U.S. won the discus-throw event and set a new Olympic record.

COLD WAR THAWS A LITTLE

April 26, London Nikita Khrushchev has been visiting Britain for talks with Prime Minister Anthony Eden. Though the East and the West cannot agree, Khrushchev said, they could respect each other's point of view. There could be "peaceful co-existence" between the two. This is seen as a softening of the Soviet hard-line policy toward the West. But in America, Secretary of State John Dulles said the United States must be prepared to go to the brink of war.

In February Khrushchev denounced Stalin. He said he was a brutal murderer. Perhaps people will be able to live happier lives now the truth is out. Some political prisoners have been freed.

Anthony Eden (left) and Khrushchev shake hands at No. 10 Downing Street.

NEWS IN BRIEF . . .

ACTRESSES MARRY

June 29, Hollywood Today glamorous film star Marilyn Monroe married the playwright Arthur Miller. His latest play, *The Crucible*, is about a witch-hunt in 17th-century America. It was first staged while Senator McCarthy was engaged on his modern witch-hunt of Communists. Marilyn Monroe is going to London to film *The Prince and the Showgirl* with British actor Lawrence Olivier.

This past April, the beautiful American actress Grace Kelly married her Prince Charming. He is Prince Rainier of Monaco, a tiny country on the Mediterranean, between France and Italy. Grace Kelly's last movie, *To Catch a Thief*, may have shown her a taste of the future. Its setting is the French Riviera.

Wedding belles: Marilyn Monroe and husband Arthur Miller, above, and below, Grace Kelly, who is now Princess of Monaco.

NEW PLAY AT EDINBURGH FESTIVAL

Sept., Edinburgh, Scotland One of Dylan Thomas's last works was a radio play called *Under Milk Wood*. It has now been made into a stage play. The play tells of a day in the life of a Welsh seashore town called Llaregub. It is full of comic, tender, and sad characters and situations. It was first heard on the radio in 1954, narrated by Richard Burton. Just three months before, Dylan Thomas had died in New York.

FIGHT FOR FRENCH WOMEN'S RIGHTS

Oct. 31, Grenoble, France A law passed 36 years ago makes family planning illegal in France. An enterprising woman is fighting the law. She has opened a birth-control clinic in Grenoble. Women have fewer rights in France than in America. A married woman even has to have her husband's permission to open a bank account.

1957

LITTLE ROCK SCHOOL TO INTEGRATE

Sept. 1, Little Rock, Ark. Children in the South have in the past attended separate schools for Negroes and whites. The Supreme Court in 1954 declared this to be unconstitutional. But change has been very slow. In the Deep South segregation is still the rule. Last year a federal court finally ordered Little Rock, Arkansas, to start integration in the 1957–1958 school year. The school board has obeyed. Nine Negro pupils are to start attending Central High School on September 3.

GOVERNOR SENDS IN THE GUARDS

Sept. 2, Little Rock Governor Orval Faubus has ordered the National Guard to surround Central High School. He claims this is to prevent violence tomorrow when nine Negro pupils are to start school. The governor's action seems to be causing problems where none existed before.

GUARDS TURN CHILDREN AWAY

Sept. 4, Little Rock None of the nine Negro pupils arrived to start school here yesterday. However, today two Negro and two white church leaders walked with the nine Negro pupils to school. The National Guard turned them away. So they walked back calmly and bravely through a huge mob of jeering whites. People from all over the country have been blaming President Eisenhower for allowing this situation to develop. They say he should be making sure that the Supreme Court's decision is enforced.

PRESIDENT SENDS IN TROOPS

Sept. 25, Little Rock Today Negro students finally succeeded in entering the high school. President Eisenhower has denounced the governor of Arkansas. He has sent 1,100 army paratroopers to Little Rock. He has also made the National Guard into a state police force. This means the governor cannot give the Guard orders.

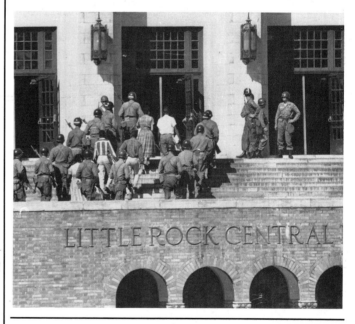

VICTORY HARD FOR NEGROES

Sept. 30, Little Rock The nine Negro pupils are showing great courage. They are escorted to and from school by soldiers. Many of their schoolmates are unkind and insulting. But they are determined to stay. The governor is furious, and many white voters are on his side. The fight for the civil rights of Negroes in the South is not yet won.

HUMPHREY BOGART DEAD

Jan. 14, Hollywood Actor Humphrey Bogart has died of throat cancer at 57. Bogart is best known for his "tough guy" roles in movies. In 1951 he won an Oscar for his part in *The African Queen*. His other movies include *The Maltese Falcon* and *Casablanca*.

Humphrey Bogart with Ingrid Bergman in *Casablanca*.

SIX COUNTRIES IN ECONOMIC UNION

March 25, Rome Six Western European nations today joined together to form a Common Market. The nations are France, West Germany, Italy, Belgium, Holland, and Luxembourg. After the tragic events in Hungary last year, they wish for a stronger western Europe. The six nations will allow their people to move freely between member countries. They will not tax one anothers' exports. They hope to increase industry and trade.

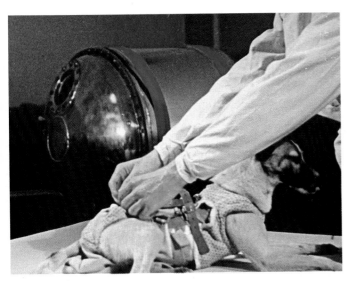

Laika is prepared for her space journey.

GOLD COAST BECOMES GHANA

March 7, Accra There were joyful celebrations in Accra tonight. The Gold Coast is the first British African colony to become an independent member of the British Commonwealth. The new president, Dr. Kwame Nkrumah, renamed the country "Ghana." (A previous Ghana in West Africa was a wealthy trading nation in the 11th century.) As the British flag came down, the new Ghanaians hoisted their own flag of red, yellow, and green.

Dr. Nkrumah in the Ghanaian Legislative Assembly.

RUSSIAN SPACE SUCCESS

Nov. 2, Moscow The Russians have launched the world's first artificial satellite. On October 4 an enormous rocket hurtled into space, carrying a sphere which is now circling the earth. It is called *Sputnik I*, and it weighs 182 lb. (83 kg).

Now the Russians have put a much larger satellite, *Sputnik II*, into orbit. It is circling the earth at about 17,280 miles (28,800 km) an hour—with a dog named Laika on board. Laika is in a sealed container. The animal receives food at regular intervals. Machines record the effects of space travel on a living animal. Other instruments are measuring the sun's radiation, and sending signals back to earth. These signals have been picked up in many parts of the world.

Western scientists are amazed that such a large satellite could be sent into orbit. It weighs over half a ton (500 kg).

NEWS IN BRIEF . . .

AMERICAN MAKES TENNIS HISTORY

July 6, Wimbledon, England Althea Gibson's life has been made up of tennis "firsts." She was born 30 years ago in Harlem, New York. In 1950 she was the first Negro player in an important tennis tournament at Forest Hills, in New York. She was the first Negro woman to win Wimbledon doubles, the French singles and doubles, and the Italian singles. And she has crowned her career this week by winning not only the singles but also the doubles championships at Wimbledon.

Miss Gibson, the number one seed at Wimbledon.

THE BEAT GENERATION

June 2, San Francisco "Beatniks" in khaki trousers, sandals, and sweaters are the in-crowd in this city. The men wear beards and the girls use heavy eyeshadow. Sometimes they smoke "pot," but they don't go in for hard drugs. They see their way of life as a new religion. They say they love everybody and everything. Their talk is full of slang: "chicks," "dig," "bread." The word "like" occurs in almost every sentence: "Like it means nothing;" "It's like cool."

SMOKING AND CANCER LINKED

June 5, Washington A committee of experts has reported that scientific evidence proves that there is a direct link between smoking and lung cancer. The panel was appointed by the American Heart Association, the National Heart and Cancer Institutes, and the American Cancer Society. Its findings call for public health measures to stop smoking.

RACING DRIVER BEATS OWN RECORD

August 4, Germany Juan Fangio has become the world car-racing champion by winning the German Grand Prix, which is the toughest circuit in Europe. On the bumpy track tires burst, mirrors fall off, and shock-absorbers become red hot. Last year Fangio drove a record lap in 9 minutes 41.6 seconds in a Lancia Ferrari. In this year's race, in a Maserati, his fastest lap was 9 minutes 17.4 seconds. Afterward Fangio said, "I took myself and my car to the limit, and perhaps a little bit more."

SPACE EXPLORATION AND ENTERTAINMENT

Sept. 26, New York Are we all space mad? Movie-makers seem to think so. We have an endless diet of science fiction, evil aliens, mad scientists, shock, and horror. The latest example is *The Incredible Shrinking Man*. It follows *Invaders from Mars* and *Invasion of the Body Snatchers*.

West Side Story, a musical now showing here, brings us back to earth, and to the present. This is the story of a modern Romeo and Juliet. Leonard Bernstein's marvelous music accompanies teenage gang warfare and a haunting love story.

A scene from *West Side Story*.

TOURISTS DISCOVER COSTA DEL SOL

July 15, Madrid, Spain Tourism is a new industry in Spain. The Spaniards did not like it at first. Many of them are poor, and resent having to serve wealthy vacationers. But tourists bring money to the country. Plots of land on the unspoiled coastal areas are selling well. The rate of exchange is very much in the tourists' favor, making food and drink there very cheap.

1958

CIVIL WAR IN ALGERIA

ALGERIANS WANT SELF-GOVERNMENT

Jan. 1, Algiers Algeria has been a French colony for a hundred years. It has a million French settlers. Most native Algerians are Muslims. Many have to migrate to France to find work. There is none for them in Algeria.

Members of a political party, the National Liberation Front (FLN), want to get rid of the French settlers. They want self-government. For four years they have been fighting the French army and the settlers.

ALGERIA TO STAY FRENCH

Feb. 5, Paris The French parliament has voted for Algeria to remain a part of the French republic. They say that both Frenchmen and Algerian Muslims should take part in the Algerian government. FLN members are totally against this. They continue to fight for independence.

ATROCITIES IN NORTH AFRICA

Feb. 12, Algiers The prime minister of neighboring Tunisia has asked French troops to leave Algeria. The French have bombed a Tunisian village just over the border. They thought FLN fighters were hiding there. The bombs killed and wounded 75 Tunisians, many of them children.

FRENCH SETTLERS SHOW STRENGTH

May 13, Algiers There are now 500,000 French soldiers in Algeria. In the guerrilla fighting, casualties on both sides have been heavy. The army and the settlers are afraid that the French government will give in to the FLN. So today they seized government buildings, and business has come to a standstill. In Paris, people have been rioting in support of the settlers.

The French government is weak, and the war in Algeria is costing France more than it can afford. The settlers want General de Gaulle to take over. They are sure he would support them.

French troops near Algiers display the stock of arms seized in a recent battle with FLN fighters, 44 of whom were killed.

DE GAULLE SPEAKS TO ALGERIA

Oct. 23, Paris General de Gaulle became premier of France in June. He has dashed the settlers' hopes of a French Algeria. He wants the country to be self-supporting, but with strong ties to France. He will see that 400,000 jobs are created for Algerians.

AMERICAN WINS SOVIET CONTEST

April 14, Moscow Van Cliburn, a 23-year-old American from Shreveport, Louisiana, has won the USSR's coveted International Tchaikovsky Piano Competition. The eight other contestants included three Russians. The tall, blond Cliburn is a favorite with Russian reporters and audiences.

Van Cliburn began to play the piano when he was 3. His mother was his first piano teacher. One of his favorite composers is Chopin.

NOBEL WINNER DENIED PRIZE

Dec. 10, Stockholm, Sweden Russian writer Boris Pasternak has been awarded the Nobel Prize for Literature. His most recent book is *Dr. Zhivago*. He could only publish it abroad, because of Russian censorship. The USSR has banned his work and will not allow him to accept the prize.

ATOMIC SUB CREW HONORED

Aug. 27, New York The crew of the nuclear submarine *Nautilus* was given a ticker-tape parade here today. Also honored was Rear Admiral Hyman Rickover. He is credited with having had a major role in the development of the Navy's nuclear submarine fleet. It had just been announced that last summer the *Nautilus* made the world's first undersea trip across the North Pole. It went right under the polar ice cap. The voyage of the *Nautilus* has great importance for U.S. defense strategy. It shows that it may be possible to launch guided missiles from submarines in the Arctic.

NEW SPACE AGENCY OPENED

July 29, Washington We are racing to catch up with the Russians in space exploration. The National Aeronautics and Space Agency (NASA) has been opened. It will carry out research on rockets and spacecraft. The U.S. has two satellites in a higher orbit than that of the Russian Sputniks. One of them is making its own electricity from sunlight. They are small satellites, and their purpose is to record data about the earth and space.

MIDDLE EASTERN CRISIS ALARMS WEST

July 14, Baghdad, Iraq Earlier this year Egypt and Syria became the United Arab Republic (UAR). Iraq and Jordan also united their two kingdoms. Now there has been a coup in Iraq. The 23-year-old King Feisal, his uncle, and his prime minister have all been murdered. Colonel Nasser of Egypt has backed the coup. King Hussein of Jordan is now afraid that the UAR, led by Nasser, may attack Jordan. The Americans and British are landing troops in Jordan. The Russians back the UAR. The two superpowers, America and the Soviet Union, are on opposite sides of a dangerous international conflict once again.

POPE WINS PRISONERS' FREEDOM

Nov. 7, Barcelona Three days ago the new pope, John XXIII, was crowned in Rome. Spain's General Franco announced that in honor of the occasion political prisoners would be released. Today over 16,000 men and women were set free and have joined their families. Many were imprisoned without a trial, and on minor charges. There is no sign that General Franco's government will change its policy.

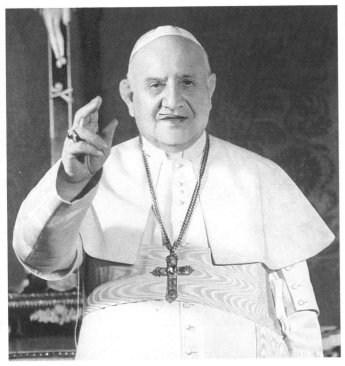

His Holiness Pope John XXIII.

KHRUSHCHEV WANTS BERLIN FREE

Nov. 30, Moscow Nikita Khrushchev has got rid of all his rivals in the Kremlin. He is now looking toward East Germany. He says Berlin should be a "free city." West Berliners dread this possibility. The city, they say, would not be free for very long. The French, British, and Americans are refusing to leave their zones of Berlin. Berlin is still an escape route for East Germans. Nearly a million have left the Communist East since 1952.

ELVIS HAS HIS MARCHING ORDERS

March 24, New York Elvis Presley has been drafted into the Army. The king of rock and roll has had his hair cut short. He can no longer wear the pink jackets and eye makeup that drive the girls wild. Friends say Elvis is just a quiet and polite country boy in an army uniform. He is also big business: his fans buy his records in millions.

Elvis Presley the rock 'n roll star.

NEWS IN BRIEF . . .

JET PLANES CARRY PASSENGERS

Oct. 26, New York Jet airlines have begun making regular passenger flights across the Atlantic. Pan American World Airlines flew its Boeing 707 from New York to Paris yesterday. The 707 began test flights in 1954. A Pan Am spokesman said regular jet passenger service would begin in two days. The jet flights take one third less time than the fastest propeller plane.

The Pan American jet *America* before it left for Paris on the first trip of the new passenger service.

CIRCLING IS GOOD FOR THE HIPS

Sept. 30, Paris It has been reported that Europeans are now enjoying our latest craze—the hula-hoop. Americans have been twirling the hoop for some time. Now the French are doing it—for fun and for exercise. Millions of the plastic rings are being sold.

In Paris's Champs-Elysées traffic came to a standstill when girls demonstrated the hula-hoop. They were dressed in bathing suits and accompanied by a country and western band!

NEW U.S. ROCKET PLANE

Oct. 15, Los Angeles Americans got their first look at a new kind of plane. The tiny, beelike X-15 rocket plane was displayed here today. The X-15 can reach altitudes between 100 and 150 miles (160 and 240 km). Its top speed is 4,500 miles (7,200 km) an hour. Vice-President Nixon spoke at the unveiling ceremony. He said the United States is now leading the Soviet Union in the race to outer space.

BEEHIVE HAIRSTYLES STAY PUT

Nov. 30, St. Louis Girls are back-combing their hair and holding it high off the forehead with plenty of hairspray. The "beehive" hairdo stays put! This style goes with pretty print dresses and high-heeled shoes.

HOPE DIAMOND GOES TO MUSEUM

Nov. 21, Washington The famous Hope diamond has been given to the Smithsonian. The huge stone is worth $1.5 million. It is said to bring bad luck in the form of death, mental illness, and financial ruin.

1959

HEADING FOR SPACE

LUNA II SPEEDS TO THE SUN

Jan. 12, Moscow The Russians have launched a rocket called *Luna II* toward the sun. It is the first rocket to escape earth's gravity. It will not return to the earth, but for some time it will send signals and information back.

NASA IS TRAINING ASTRONAUTS

May 28, Washington NASA is training seven men for the exciting but frightening task of being sent into space. The men will be called "astronauts." In specially designed chambers they are finding out what it is like to be weightless. They will not be sent into space until more tests are made with animal passengers. Today two monkeys returned safely after a 300-mile (480-km) journey into space.

ANOTHER "FIRST" FOR USSR

Oct. 27, Moscow This evening viewers of Moscow television saw the first extraordinary pictures of the other side of the moon—the side we never see. A Russian satellite, *Luna III*, was launched on October 4. Two days later it began to orbit the moon. A camera on the satellite took pictures for 40 minutes, and transmitted them to earth. Many of these pictures have been printed in the world's newspapers today. Russian scientists have already named eight features on the moon's far side.

DALAI LAMA SAFE IN INDIA

April 19, Lhasa, Tibet The Buddhist ruler of Tibet, the Dalai Lama, has been forced to leave his capital city, Lhasa, in disguise. When the Chinese marched into Tibet they promised to modernize the country, then leave. That was nine years ago, and they are still here. They have ruled the Tibetans harshly. Tibetan guerrillas are fighting the Chinese in the east. They have blown up bridges and mined roads. Chinese soldiers were told to capture the Dalai Lama dead or alive, but they were too late. He has arrived safely in India. His successor, the Panchen Lama, has agreed to cooperate with the Chinese.

The disguised Dalai Lama escapes from Tibet in the dark robes of a servant.

CUBA FREED FROM DICTATOR

REJOICING IN HAVANA

Jan. 2, Havana, Cuba There has been a coup in Cuba, and President Batista has fled to the Dominican Republic. He has ruled Cuba, an island in Central America, as the cruel dictator of a police state for many years. Since he came to power the rich have become richer. Havana is full of Cadillacs, luxury houses, and gambling casinos. But most Cubans are penniless and many are actually starving. There are few jobs, no unemployment benefits, and no health care.

The coup was led by a young lawyer, Fidel Castro. He rode into Havana yesterday on a tank. His second-in-command is an Argentinian doctor, Che Guevara. In 1956 they began their guerrilla attacks from the mountains. In two and a half years their small band of adventurers has become a national movement. There was great rejoicing all over Cuba today that Batista's rule has ended.

Fidel Castro, the leader of the coup in Cuba.

CASTRO WELCOMED IN WASHINGTON

April 15, Washington Fidel Castro has been given a great welcome on his arrival for talks with the Vice-President. The United States is pleased that he will hold free elections in Cuba. Castro was sworn in as prime minister in February. Manuel Urrutia is the president.

THE U.S. THINKS AGAIN

July 18, Havana The United States is now worried that Castro is going too far. He has dismissed Urrutia and made himself president of Cuba. He is dividing large sugar estates and distributing the land to Cuban farmers. Many of these estates belong to Americans. The United States has controlled Cuba's economy in the past, importing two thirds of Cuba's sugar at fixed prices. Castro seems to be moving toward communism. He is also executing ex-president Batista's supporters after speedy trials.

MORE TROUBLE IN VIETNAM

July 9, Saigon, South Vietnam Communists in South Vietnam have rebelled against the republican government. The Communists are supported by the Viet Cong (forces of the Viet Minh) in North Vietnam. Today they killed two American soldiers. The South Vietnamese army is being trained by the United States.

PEACE IN SIGHT FOR CYPRUS

Dec. 14, Nicosia Both Greeks and Turks in Cyprus are hoping for peace at last. The British are leaving the country. They have allowed Archbishop Makarios to return from exile, and today he has become president of a new independent Cyprus. His vice-president is Turkish. Colonel Grivas has disbanded EOKA and left for Greece. After four years of bitter fighting, both sides pray that Greeks and Turks will be able to forget their differences and live peacefully together.

KHRUSHCHEV MEETS EISENHOWER

Sept. 20, Los Angeles Five days ago Nikita Khrushchev stepped out of his Russian plane, the most advanced jet Americans had ever seen. He is visiting the United States for two weeks. In Washington, he presented President Eisenhower with a model of a rocket. The real rocket had landed on the moon only a few hours earlier. The President was a little taken aback by this reminder of the Russians' success in space!

Russian leader Nikita Khrushchev with President Eisenhower, during Khrushchev's visit.

KENYA'S EMERGENCY ENDS

Nov. 10, Nairobi The Mau Mau rebellion is over. Hundreds of forest fighters have been captured. About 10,000 Mau Mau have been killed. They in turn killed about 2,000 Kikuyu civilians, 1,000 government troops, and 58 Europeans and Asians. The land question, which started the terrorist attacks, is being looked into by the government.

NEWS IN BRIEF . . .

"THE BRAIN" WAS CHEATING

Nov. 2, New York Carl Van Doren will resign from his teaching job at Columbia University. This handsome and popular man has admitted that he won $129,000 dishonestly. In the TV quiz show "Twenty-One" he answered the hardest questions, week after week. He was as popular as a movie star all over America. But one of his rivals spilled the beans. It seems that the most popular quiz competitors were shown the answers in advance. Other competitors who were shown the answers include an 11-year-old girl who won $32,000.

ISLANDS OF HAWAII BECOME OUR FIFTIETH STATE

Aug. 21, Washington Today Hawaii becomes the 50th state of the United States. The beautiful Pacific island chain is the second new state to join the Union this year. On January 3, Alaska became our 49th state. This area, rich in natural resources, was originally bought from Russia for just a couple of pennies per acre. Our new state of Alaska is twice as big as Texas, but it has fewer people than any other state. Hawaii is made up of 132 islands, but its people live only on seven of them.

Hawaii celebrated when statehood was announced.

PEOPLE OF THE FIFTIES

Hyman G. Rickover, American admiral 1900–1986

Hyman George Rickover was born in Russia. He came to the United States when he was four years old. He became an ensign in the U.S. Navy in 1922. When he retired, Rickover was a full admiral. He is best known for developing the U.S.S. *Nautilus*, the first nuclear-powered submarine, for the United States. He went on to direct the construction of the entire United States nuclear-powered Navy. Rickover started his work in the field of nuclear power in 1947. In 1965, he was given the Enrico Fermi Medal, our country's most important science award.

Rickover reached retirement age in 1964. However, his term of duty was extended. He remained active in the Navy's nuclear propulsion program until he retired in 1982.

David Ben-Gurion, Israeli prime minister 1886–1973

David Ben-Gurion was the first prime minister of the state of Israel. He served as prime minister and minister of defense from 1948 to 1953, and from 1955 to 1963. He had worked tirelessly for the formation of a Jewish state in Palestine, which had been under British control since 1918. He planned for Israel to be a homeland for Jews from anywhere in the world who wanted to come.

In 1948, Ben-Gurion proclaimed Israel's independence. He led his nation during several Arab-Israeli wars fought to stay independent.

Agatha Christie, novelist 1890–1976

The detective story writer Agatha Christie is as well known here in America as she is in her native England. She is particularly noted for her clever plots. Her two most famous characters are the Belgian private detective Hercule Poirot and the elderly village spinster Miss Jane Marple. They appeared in dozens of her detective novels. Agatha Christie's play *The Mousetrap* was on stage in London, continuously for 40 years. *Murder on the Orient Express* and *Death on the Nile* have each been filmed twice. She wrote 83 books and 16 plays during her long career.

Jomo Kenyatta, Kenyan politician 1894–1978

His real name was Kamau wa Ngengi. He grew up in a Kikuyu village at the time when the British started to colonize Kenya. He went to a mission school, and could speak English well. He spent two years in Moscow, and 20 years in London. He studied anthropology, and wrote a book about the Kikuyu people, *Facing Mount Kenya*.

In 1946 he returned to Kenya, and became head of the Kenya African Union. He was a very powerful speaker. He wanted Africans to have equal opportunities with whites. In 1953 the British accused him of leading Mau Mau terrorists. He was imprisoned for nine years. In 1964 he became president of an independent Kenya. He was immensely popular. Everyone called him "Mzee" (Elder, or Old One). Under his presidency, Kenya had a free press, and good health and education services.

Eva (Evita) Perón 1919–1952

Eva Perón was born in a tiny village, but grew to be the most influential person in Argentina. She was an actress before she married Juan Perón in 1945. She campaigned tirelessly for her husband, especially among the poorer people. With the money she raised, Eva Perón was able to increase workers' pay and open hundreds of new schools and hospitals. In 1949 Eva Perón formed a feminist movement, and persuaded her husband to change the law so as to allow women to vote. She fell ill, and three years later died of cancer. Thousands of Argentinians mourned for Eva Perón. They called her a saint.

Elvis Presley, American singer 1935–1977

Elvis grew up in Mississippi. He often heard rhythm and blues and gospel music sung by black singers, and he imitated them. One day in 1954, a recording company wanted to hire a white singer who could sound like a black singer. Elvis was exactly what they were looking for. Two years later he released "Heartbreak Hotel," the first of 45 recordings that sold over a million copies. Elvis changed the whole art of pop singing. After two years in the army he was back in show business, but the strain was beginning to tell. He put on weight, and took drugs. He died in the huge house he had bought in Memphis, Tennessee.

Grace Kelly, (Princess Grace of Monaco) 1929–1982

Grace Kelly was born in Philadelphia, Pennsylvania. When her schooldays were over she studied drama, and was soon playing in films opposite well-known actors, including Gary Cooper and Clark Gable. When she played Bing Crosby's wife in *Country Girl* (1954), she received an Academy Award for best actress. The great director Alfred Hitchcock chose her to be his leading lady in *Dial M for Murder* (1954), and *To Catch a Thief* (1955). He said she had the elegance and appeal he wanted.

On April 19, 1956 her life changed. She married Prince Rainier II, the ruler of the little state of Monaco on the Mediterranean coast. They had three children. Her death was quite unexpected. She was driving with her younger daughter on a winding hilly road in the south of France. She had a stroke, and the car plunged down an embankment.

Ernesto Guevara de la Serna (Che Guevara) 1928–1967

"Che" Guevara was an Argentinian, an athlete, a scholar, and a medical doctor. But he devoted his life to fighting corrupt regimes. He felt that people in underdeveloped countries should struggle to be free of dictatorship and poverty. He met Fidel Castro in Mexico, and together they went to Cuba. They led the guerrillas against Batista's government. Che Guevara became a Cuban citizen when Castro took power, and served in his government. In the 1960s he joined Patrice Lumumba's national movement in the Congo (Central Africa). When that failed he became a guerrilla leader in Bolivia. In 1967 he was captured by government forces there, and shot.

American Firsts

1950   Ralph J. Bunche became first black American to
win the Nobel Peace Prize.
The first National Book Awards were given: *The
Man with the Golden Arm* by Nelson Algren
won for fiction.
CBS was issued the first license to begin color
TV broadcasting.
First NBA basketball championships were won
by the Minneapolis Lakers.

1951   First electrical power from atomic energy was
obtained, Idaho Falls, Ind.
First coast-to-coast direct-dial phone service was
inaugurated.
First telecast of an opera written for TV was
produced—*Amahl and the Night Visitors*, New
York City.

1952   Franklin National Bank, of Franklin Square,
N.Y., issued the first bank credit cards.
Nylon stretch yarn was introduced.
C.A. Bass became first black woman to be
nominated for vice-presidency.

1953   Photographic type-composing machine
exhibited, Chicago.
Oscar ceremonies telecast for first time.

1954   Gas-turbine auto was exhibited, NYC
Hydraulic-lift parking device was installed,
Washington, D.C.
Linus Pauling became the first person to receive
two Nobel prizes.
Tissue bank for storage of human tissue grafts
was begun, Bethesda, Md.

1955   First auto seat belt safety legislation was
enacted, Ill.
Salk polio vaccine was developed.
First televised press conference by a President
was filmed.

1956   Magnetic tape recorder of sound and pictures for
television was demonstrated.
First successful in-flight refueling of a helicopter
accomplished, Ft. Rucker, Ala.

| 1957 | Synthetic amino acids manufactured. Electric portable typewriters placed on sale, Syracuse, N.Y. |

| 1958 | Solid-state electronic computer developed, Philadelphia, Pa. Bifocal contact lenses introduced, Chicago, Ill. First two-way moving sidewalk in service, Dallas, Tex. |

| 1959 | Saint Lawrence Seaway completed. Color photo of earth from outer space taken by missile launched at Cape Canaveral, Fla. Synthetic penicillin developed. Atomic submarines equipped with Polaris underwater missiles. |

New words and expressions

The English language is always changing. New words are added to it, and old words are used in new ways. New inventions, habits, and occupations cause people to introduce new words. Some of them are included in this list of words and expressions that first appeared or came into popular use in the 1950s.

Asian flu
bailout
big daddy
brainstorm
bumper-to-bumper
class action
cool
death row
deep-six
desegregation
dig it
downshift
drip-dry
flight attendant
free world
gal Friday
high-rise
hippy

lip sync
Little League
McCarthyism
miracle drug
monkey bars
one-upmanship
overachiever
party pooper
press secretary
red alert
rhythm and blues
rock and roll
skydiving
snowblower
splashdown
square
talent show
voice-over

How many of these words and expressions do we still use today? Do you know what they all mean?

Glossary

abdicate: to give up a throne

abduct: to kidnap

anonymous: not identified or named

anthropology: the study of human beings

become extinct: die out forever

boycott: an organized agreement to refuse to have anything to do with a company, person, or organization; usually until certain conditions are met

campaign: run for public office

coexistence: living together, usually in peace

corrupt: morally wrong or improper

Cypriot: a native of Cyprus

denounce: accuse or criticize publicly

depose: remove from a throne

discrimination: prejudiced outlook, treatment, or acts; usually based on race or religion

fossil: remains of an animal or plant that has been preserved, and is still recognizable

guerrilla fighters: people who fight independently; not in the regular army

Kremlin: fortified part of a Russian town; in this case, the place in Moscow where the government officially meets

mud flat: stretch of mud by river or sea, uncovered at low tide

nuclear scientist: someone working on atomic projects

oath: a solemn promise

orbit: to circle or revolve around, as the path of a satellite around a planet

pact: agreement, treaty

paratroops: soldiers who are dropped by parachute

pilgrim: a person who makes a special journey to a holy place

radioactive: atomic explosions cause "radioactivity," or a change in the structure of a cell. If cells in a human body are affected, the person becomes permanently ill.

satellite: a natural or artificial object that goes around the earth or other celestial body—the moon is a natural satellite

segregation: the enforced separation of a race, class, or ethnic group from others

transient labor: people who travel in search of work and are hired for a short time, usually for seasonal employment

USSR/Soviet Union: These names refer to the same country (now generally referred to as Russia).

veto: forbid, reject

Further Reading

Cairns, Trevor. *The Twentieth Century.* Lerner, 1984

Carey, Helen and Greenberg, Judith. *How to Read a Newspaper.* Watts, 1983

——*How to Use Primary Sources.* Watts, 1983

Crocker, Chris. *Great American Astronauts.* Watts, 1988

Darby, Jean. *Dwight D. Eisenhower.* Lerner, 1989

Faber, Doris and Faber, Harold. *Martin Luther King, Jr.* Messner, 1986

Finkelstein, Norman. *The Emperor General: A Biography of Douglas MacArthur.* Macmillan, 1989

Friese, Kai J. *Rosa Parks: The Movement Organizes.* Silver Burdett Press, 1990

Graham, Ian. *Attack Submarine.* Watts, 1989

Jarrett, William. *Timetables of Sports History: The Olympic Games.* Facts on File, 1990

Pascoe, Elaine. *Racial Prejudice.* Watts, 1985

Silverstein Herma. *David Ben-Gurion.* Watts, 1988

Smith, Carter. *The Korean War.* Silver Burdett Press, 1990

Stacy, Tom. *The Fifties.* Raintree Steck-Vaughn, 1990

Tames, Richard. *Nineteen Fifties.* Watts, 1990

Tedards, Anne. *Marian Anderson.* Chelsea House, 1988

Index